Table of Contents

About the Author 2
How to Use This Book 3
Guitar Types 4
The Parts of the Guitar 5
Playing Position 6
The Pick and the Strings 7
Finger Fun 8
Tuning 9
The Staff 10
Tablature 11
Electric 12
The Whole Note 13
The Count 14
Famous 15
F Slide 16
The Quarter Rest 17
Quarters and Gumballs 18
Gila Monster 19
The Half Note 20
Name These Notes 21
G-Wiggle 22
Mix It Up 23
Animal Crackers 24
Sand Dollars & Shark Teeth 25
Bologna Sandwich 26
The Musical Alphabet 27
Catfish 28
The Pull-Off 29
Super Duper Note Review 30
Test Your Knowledge 31
Note Legend 32
Congratulations! 33

About the Author

Kelly Weeks is a talented, young and energetic musician who began his musical career as a singer/songwriter, playing solo and with bands in the Minneapolis, Boston and Orlando areas. After completing his Bachelor's degree in Professional Music from the Berklee College of Music, Kelly went on to provide private lessons to students of all ages in his home town of Minneapolis in 2003. In order to further his teaching and musical abilities, Kelly completed a K-12 Instrumental Teaching License from Hamline University, and his Master's degree in Instrumental Education in 2012.

Kelly has extensive experience teaching students of varying levels and needs in both the public school system and in private settings. In addition, Kelly is an accomplished songwriter, whose songs can currently be heard on various MTV shows as well as The Young and the Restless.

How to Use This Book

Kasey's Guitar Method for Kids is a book designed for children ages 4-9. It is a fun way and engaging way for children to learn how to read music and play basic guitar techniques.

Throughout the book there are icons next to activities such as "Draw" or "Play." These activities allow the young student to learn in different ways. Many of the songs in the book have play-along recordings online.

These recordings can be found at
http://kellysmusicbooks.com/media

These recordings are the core focus of this book. Have your child/student listen and play-along with them. Have fun!

Guitar Types

There are two types of guitars: acoustic and electric.
You can use either type for this book.

Guitars come in many different shapes and sizes. Circle your favorite guitar.

The Parts of the Guitar

TUNERS
FRETS
NECK*
STRINGS
BODY
BRIDGE

*Daniels far part of the guitar is the neck.

Playing Position

STANDING POSITION If you practice standing up it is strongly recommended that you use a shoulder strap to keep the guitar in the correct position. The height at which the guitar hangs from your shoulder should position the guitar at about belly button level or a little higher. It should hang down in front of your body and be closer to side of your strumming hand. The angle of the guitar should position the tuners higher than the body of the guitar. The neck of the guitar should not be parallel with the ground.

SEATED POSITION The strap is not as important as in the seated position but it is still highly recommended. If you are right handed then the guitar should sit on your right thigh. The guitar should balance on your thigh so that it is not supported by your left hand. Position the guitar so that it angles the head stock up slightly. The guitar should be held secure under your strumming hand arm. If a strap is used in the seated position it should position the guitar in the same way as it was in the standing position.

The Pick and the Strings

TECHNIQUE

HOLD THE PICK
Hold the pick between your thumb and forefinger.

PRESS DOWN THE STRING
Use the tip of your finger to press down on the string. Use your thumb to squeeze the neck of your guitar.

Finger Fun

Trace your fretting hand, and write in the finger numbers!

Tuning

This book uses standard tuning. This means that your guitar strings should be tuned like the picture here.

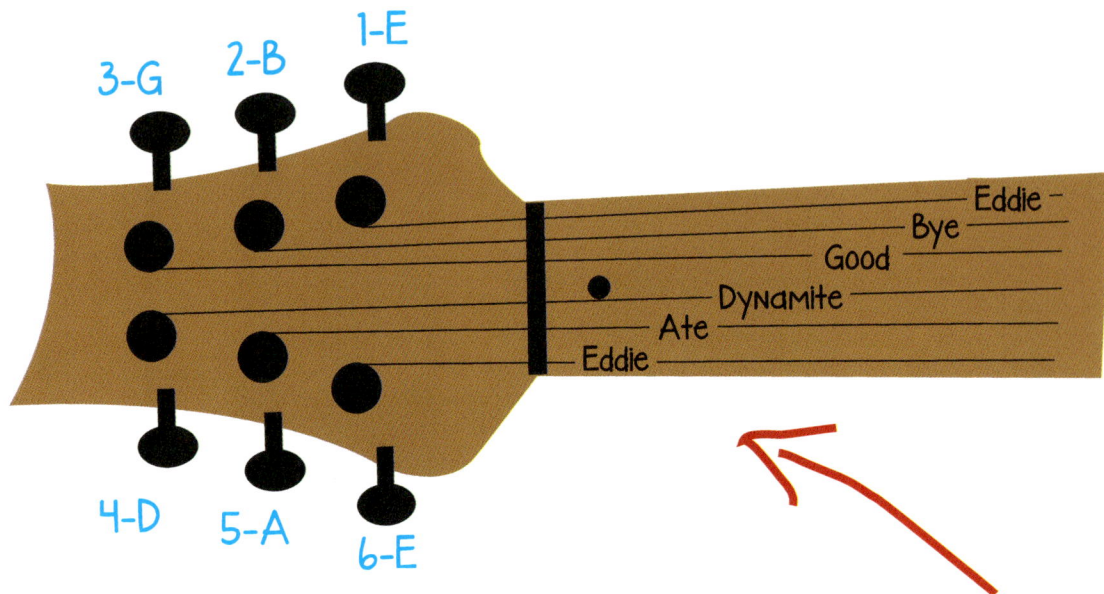

To remember this sequence say "Eddie-Ate-Dynamite-Good-Bye-Eddie."

Electronic Tuner

The best way to tune your guitar is with an electronic tuner. You should invest some money in an electronic tuner. It will make tuning much easier for you.

The Staff

The staff is what's used to learn music

Notes are written on the staff. It tells us what to play.

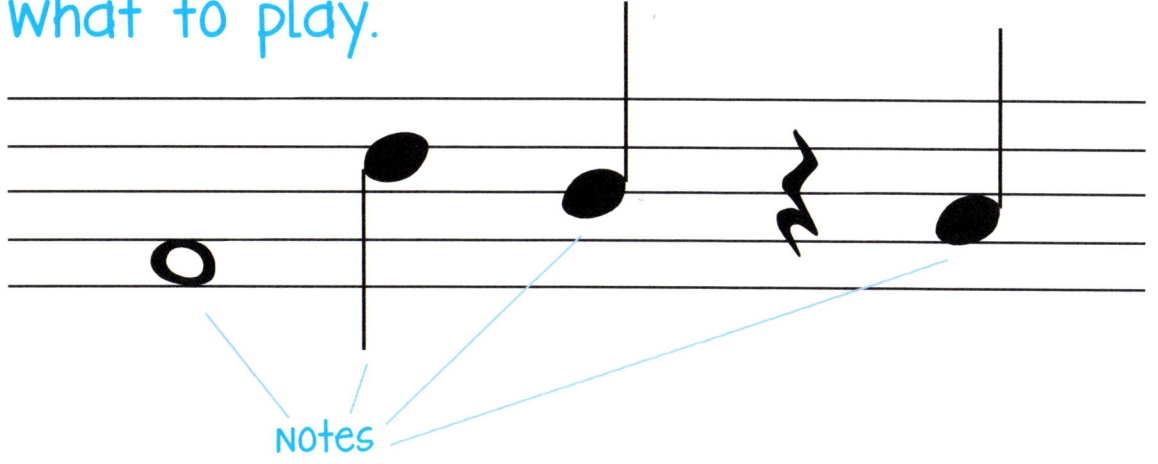
notes

There are many symbols in music. Here are several you will see in this book.

Treble Clef   Time Signature   Rest   Repeat Sign

Tablature

Tablature is the written form of notation that is widely used for the guitar. In a nutshell, tablature indicates the location of a note on the fret board. Tablature shows six lines which represent the six strings on the guitar. The top line represents the first string, which is the string on the guitar that is closest to the floor as you hold it, also known as the high E string. The bottom line represents the sixth string, which is the thickest string in diameter. The 4/4 at the beginning of the song is called a time signature. This indicates that in each measure there are four beats and that a quarter is what is used to count the beat. The two dots at the end of this tablature example tell you to repeat back to the beginning and play the song again.

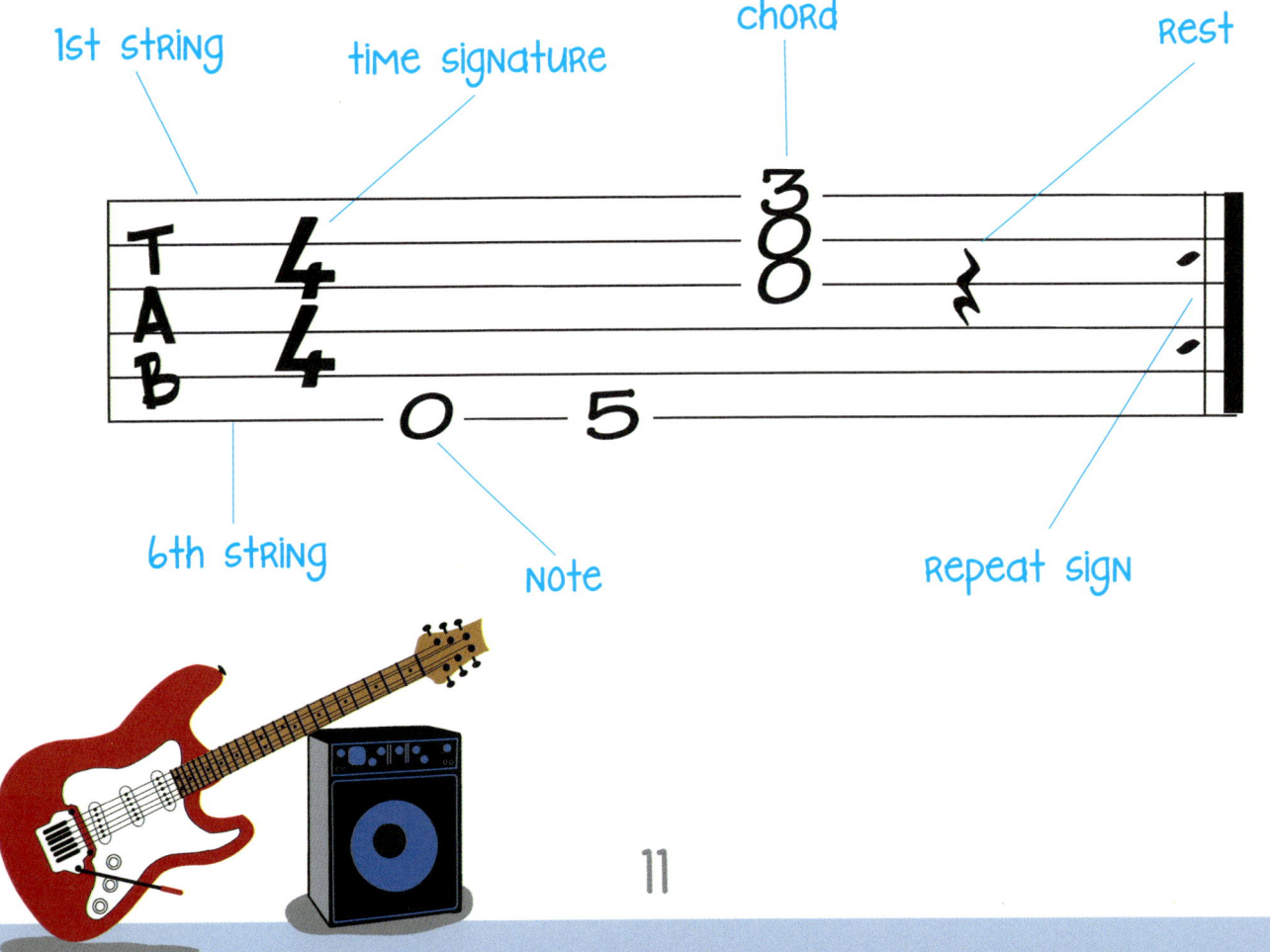

Electric

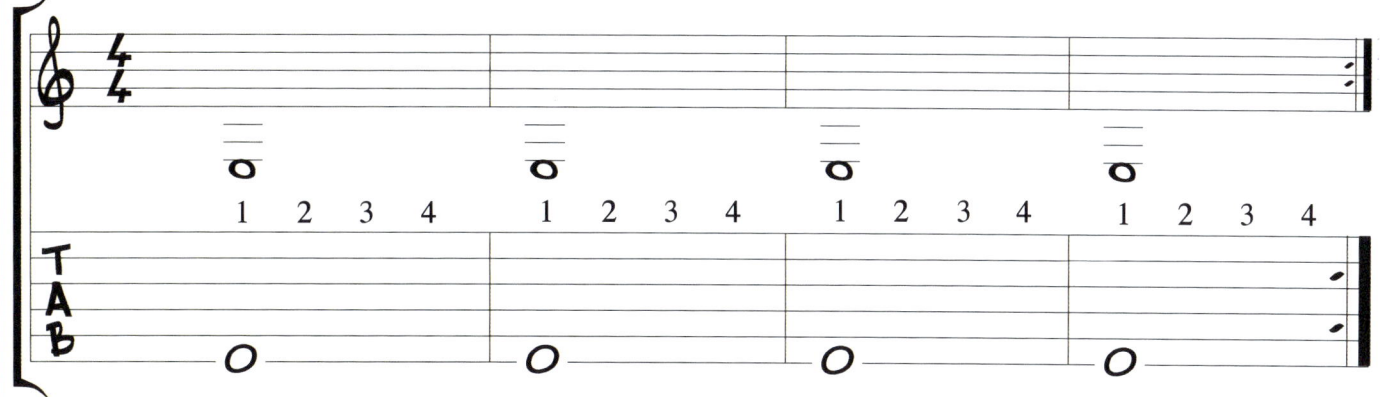

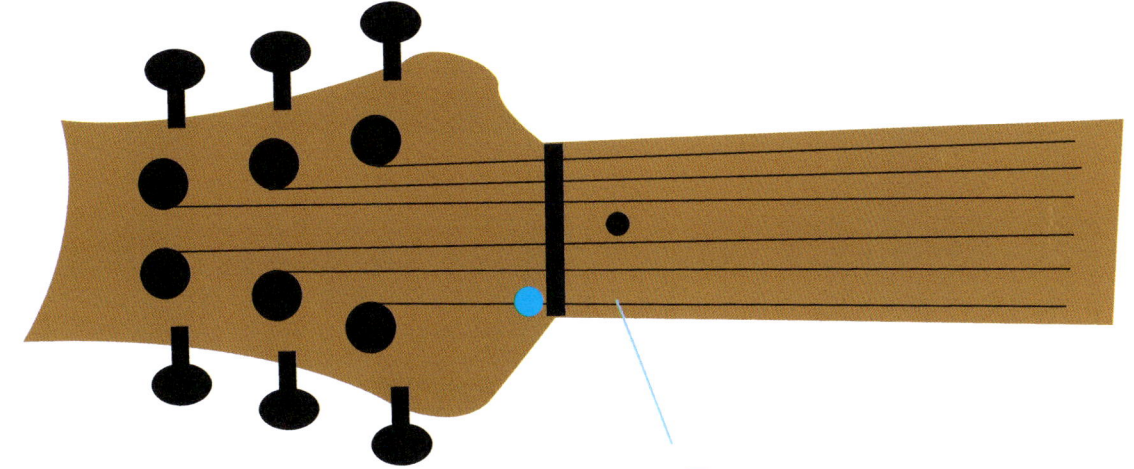

E is the open 6th string

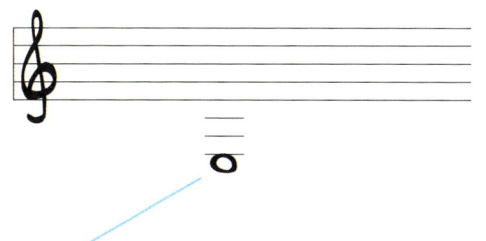

"E" is three lines and a space below the staff

This music symbol is a repeat sign. When you see it, return to the beginning of the song, and play it again.

The Whole Note

 A whole note receives four beats. When you play a whole note, count 1-2-3-4.

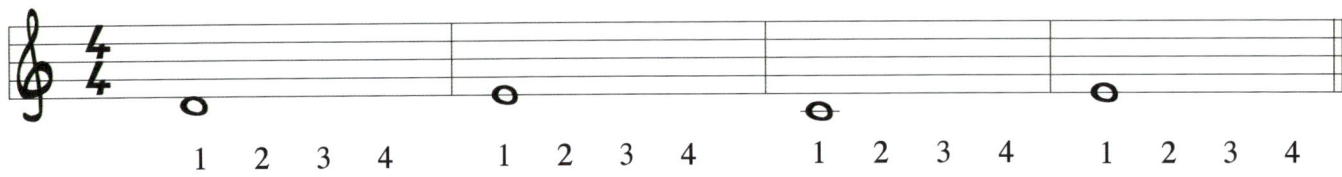

 Draw Whole Notes

Write in the counting

Most guitars are made of wood, even bright, colorful electric guitars. Their bright colors are paint that is on top of solid wood.

Famous

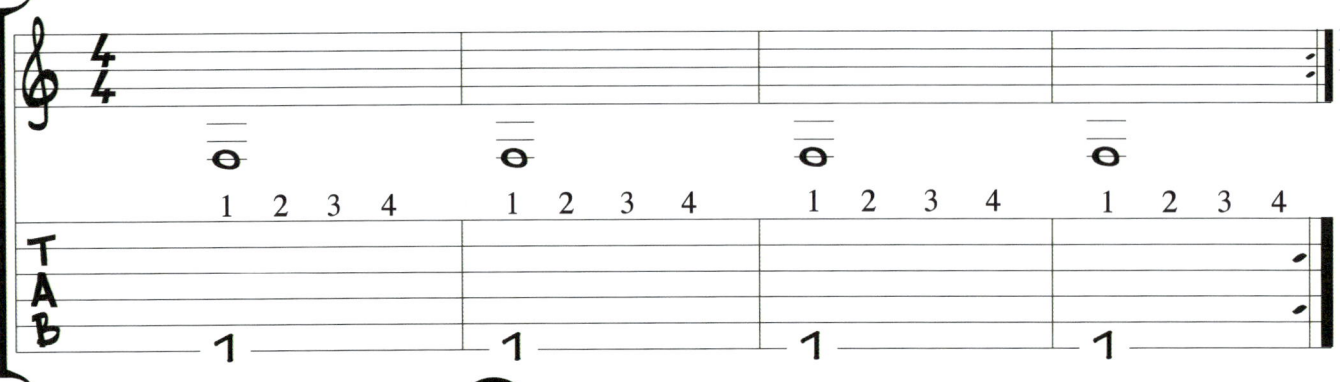

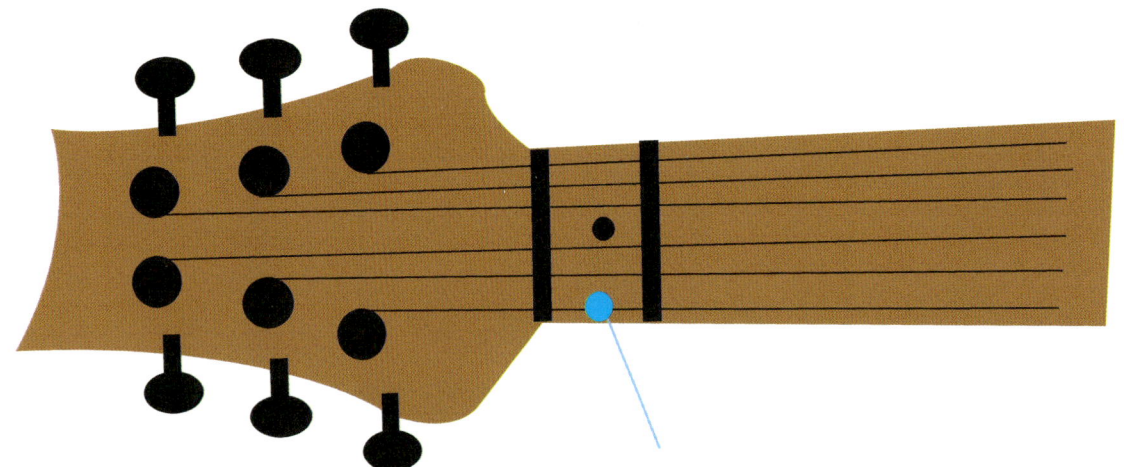

"F" is on the first fret sixth string

"F" is three lines below the staff

Use your 1st (pointer) finger to play "F."

F Slide

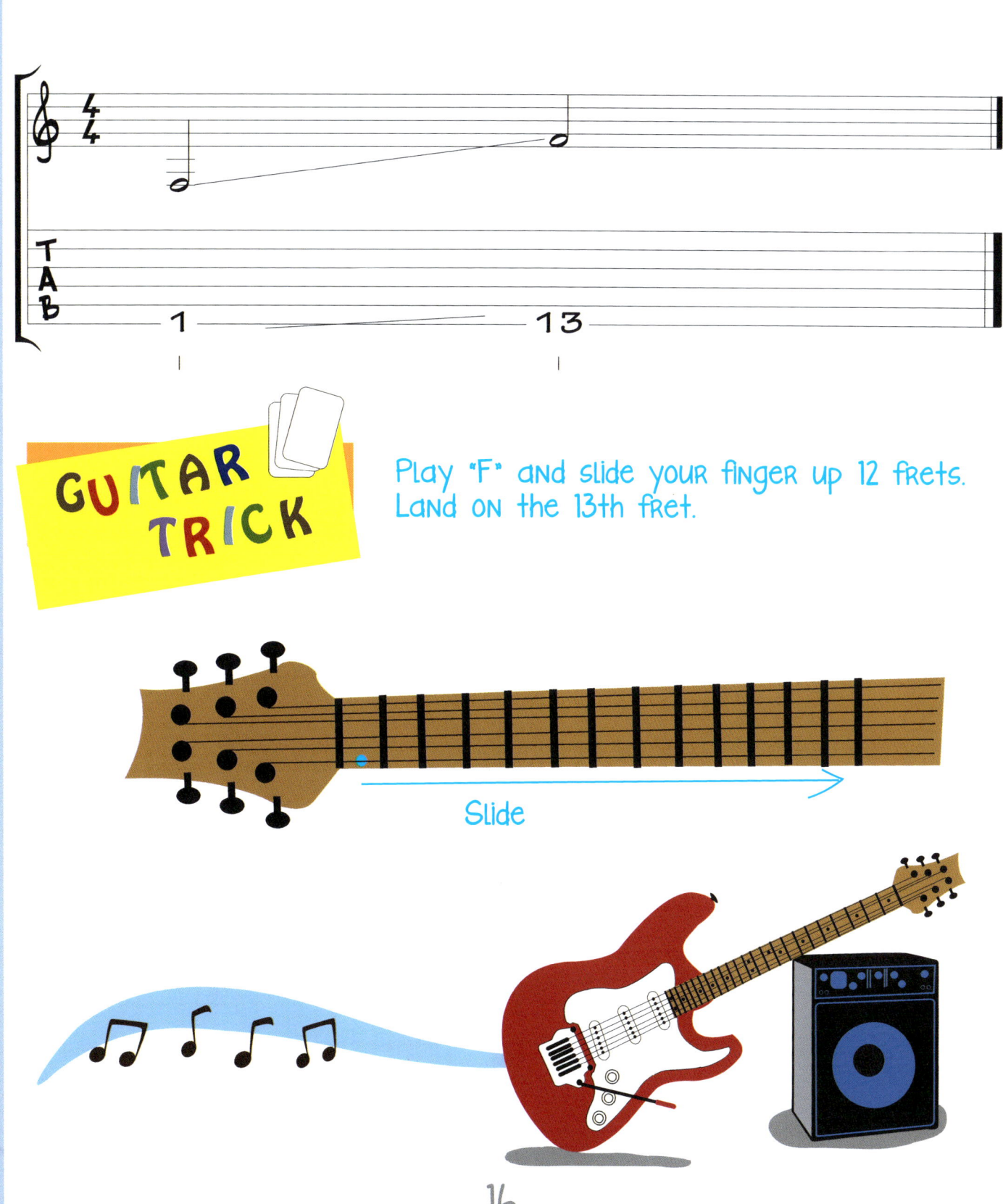

Guitar Trick: Play "F" and slide your finger up 12 frets. Land on the 13th fret.

The Quarter Rest

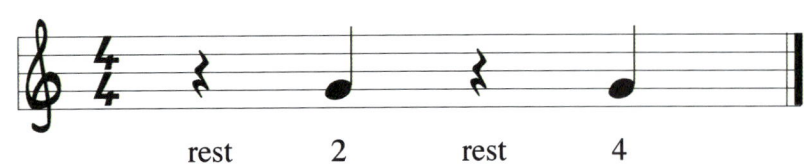

rest   2   rest   4

The Quarter Rest receives one beat of silence. When you see it, rest your hand on the string and silence it for one beat.

Draw Quarter Rests

Quarters and Gumballs

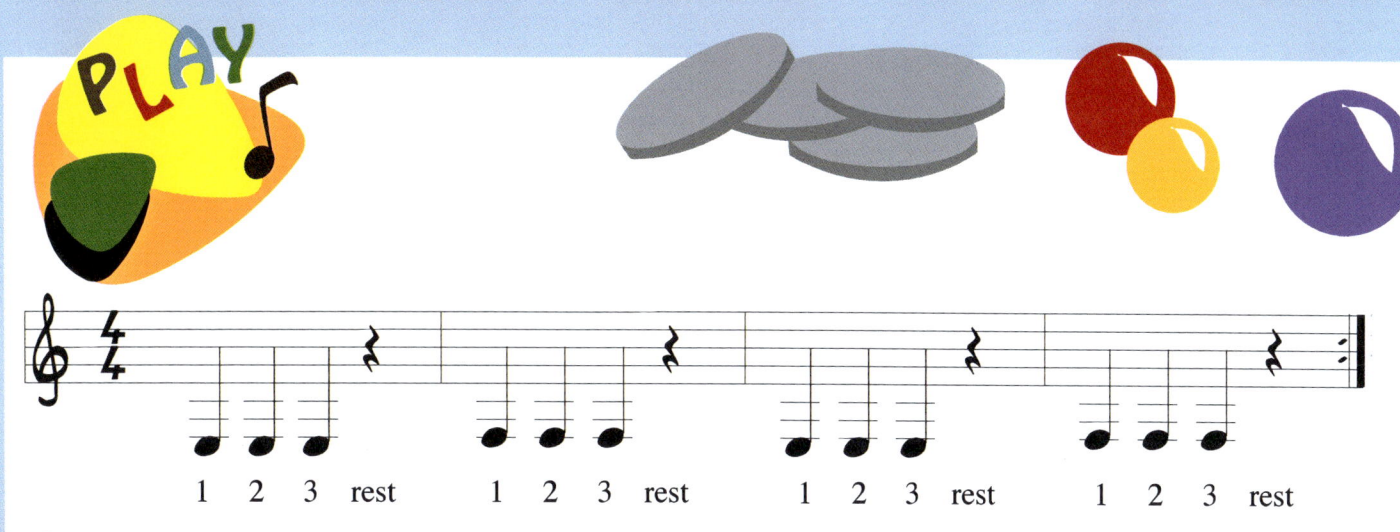

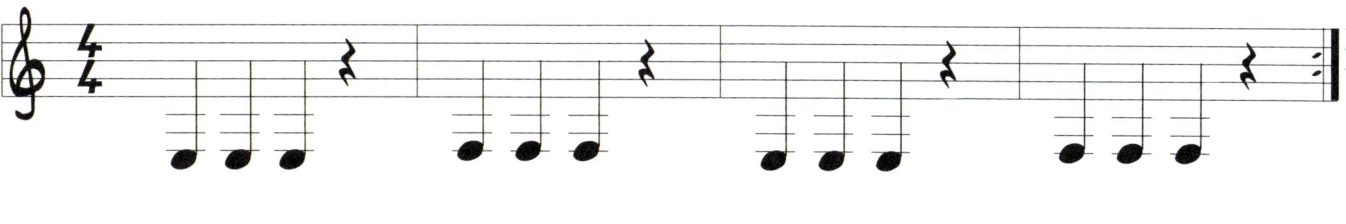

Write in the counting

Guitars have many frets. How many frets does your guitar have?

The Half Note

The half note receives two beats. When you play half notes, count two beats for each note.

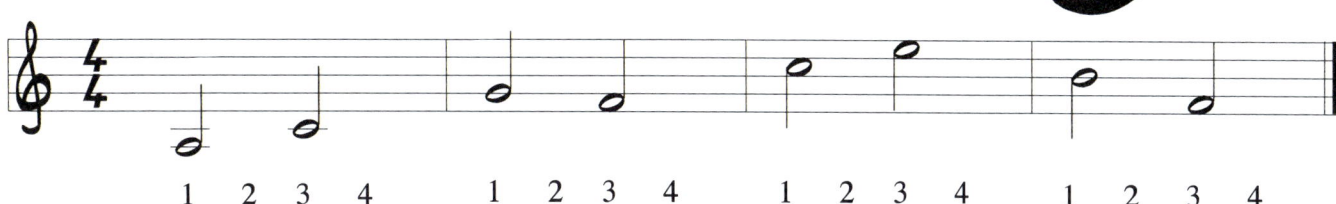

1 2 3 4   1 2 3 4   1 2 3 4   1 2 3 4

Draw Half Notes

| 1 2 3 4 | | | | |

Write in the counting

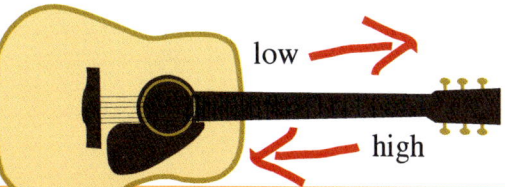

Low numbered frets like 1, 3 or 4 have lower sounds. High numbered frets like 8, 10, or 12 have higher sounds. Can you make some low sounds? Now, make some high sounds.

Name These Notes

Write in the names of the notes in the spaces above.

Note Legend "Mini"

G-Wiggle

Wiggling the strings is called vibrato. When you play "G," bend down on the string and then release it back up. Now do it quickly. That's a wiggle!

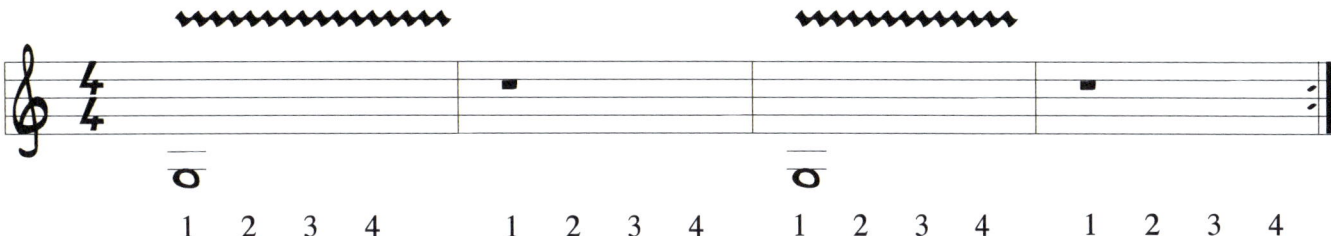

The Whole Rest

The whole rest receives four beats of silence. When you see it, rest your hand on the strings, and silence them for four beats.

Mix It Up

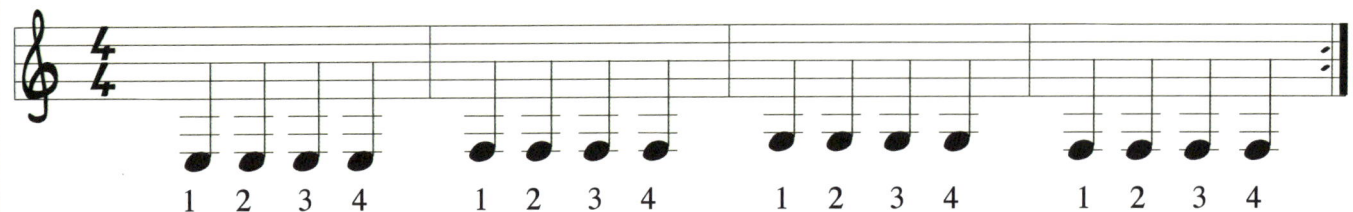

Write the letter E, F or G in each box, then play your creation.

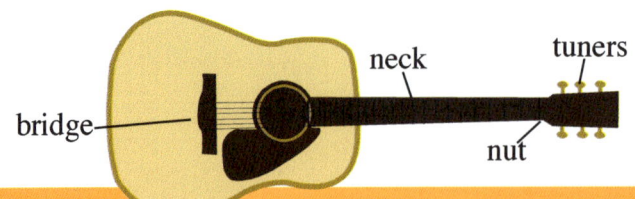

Your guitar will sound different if you pick it in different places. Try picking by the bridge for a brighter sound. Now, pick right by the neck. For fun, pick the strings by the tuners.

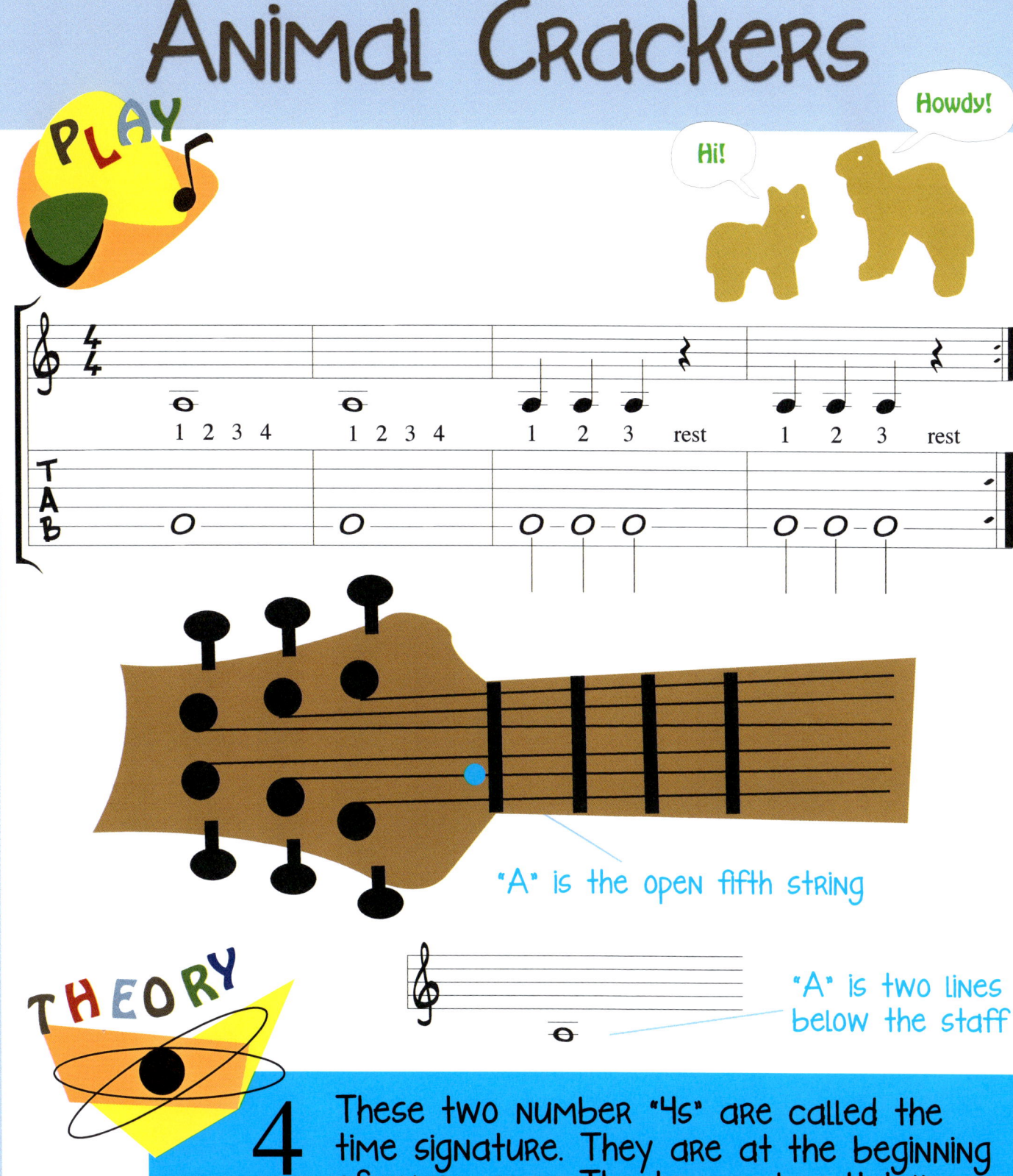

Sand Dollars & Shark Teeth

Play "A" two ways!

The note "A" is the open fifth string. This same note can also be played on the fifth fret, sixth string.

Bologna Sandwich

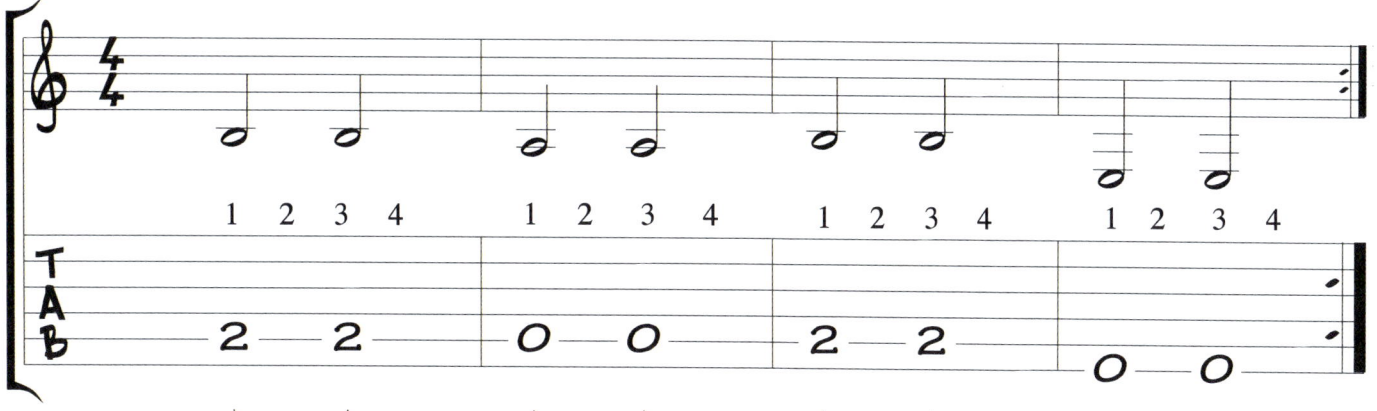

"B" is on the second fret, fifth string

"B" is one line and a space below the staff

Use your second (middle) finger to play "B"

The Musical Alphabet

THEORY

The musical alphabet only includes letters:

A, B, C, D, E, F, G

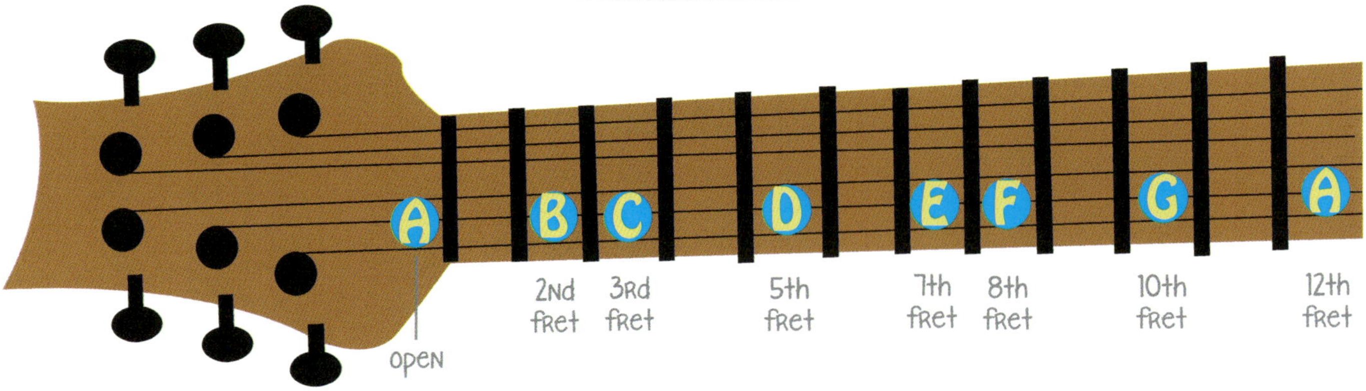

You can play the musical alphabet on your guitar by playing the letters shown in the picture. All notes are on the 5th string.

Catfish

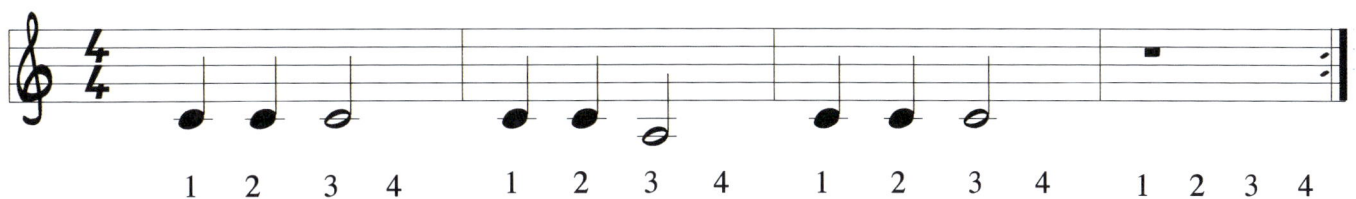

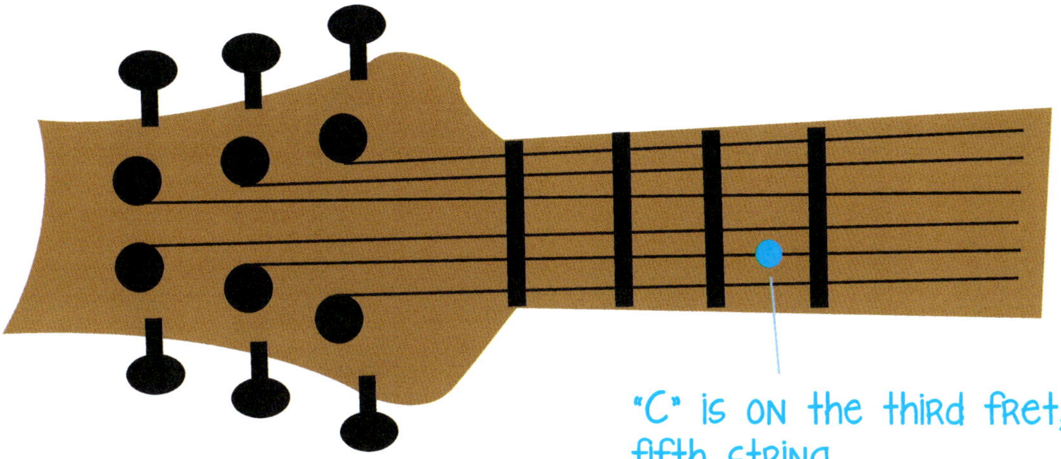

1 2 3 4   1 2 3 4   1 2 3 4   1 2 3 4

"C" is on the third fret, fifth string

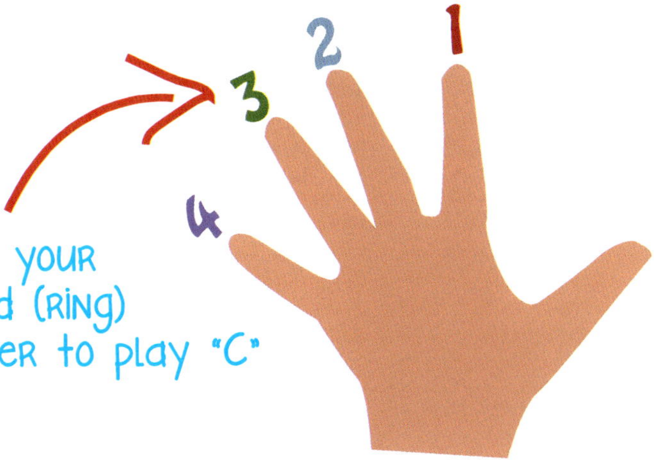

Use your third (ring) finger to play "C"

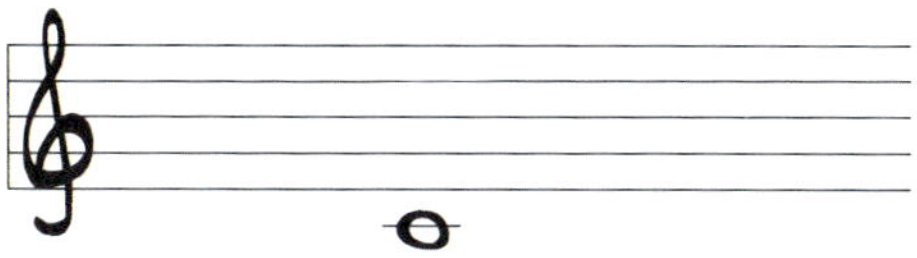

"C" is one line below the staff

28

The Pull-Off

GUITAR TRICK

A pull-off is when you play a fretted note, and then pull-off the string with your fretting finger. When you pull-off the string it will sound a new note.

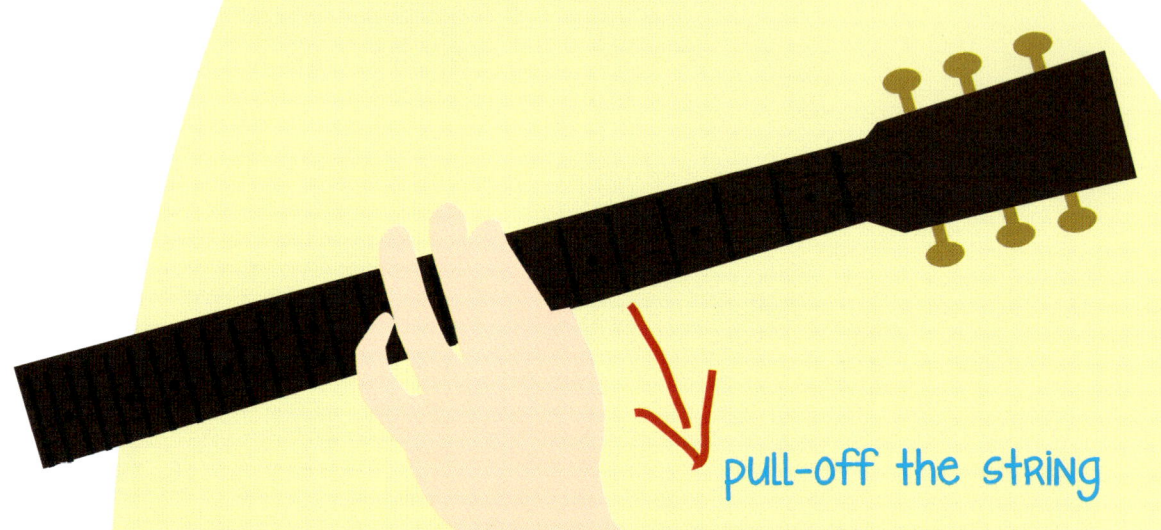

pull-off the string

Pull-offs can be played in many places. Try playing these pull-offs.

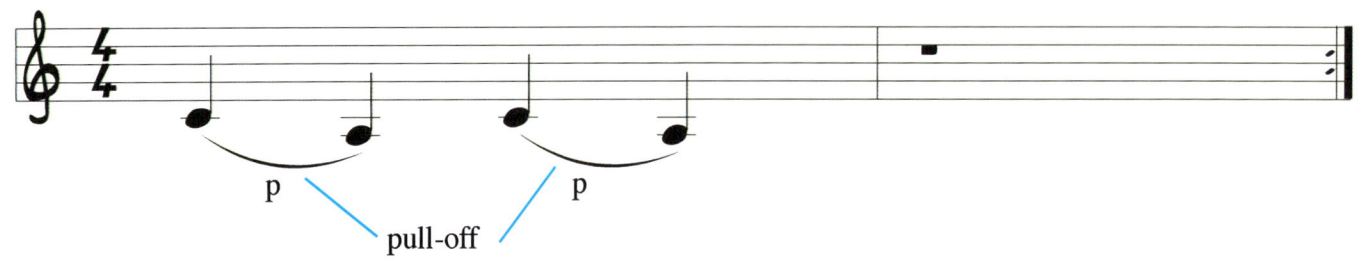

p   p
pull-off

Super Duper Note Review

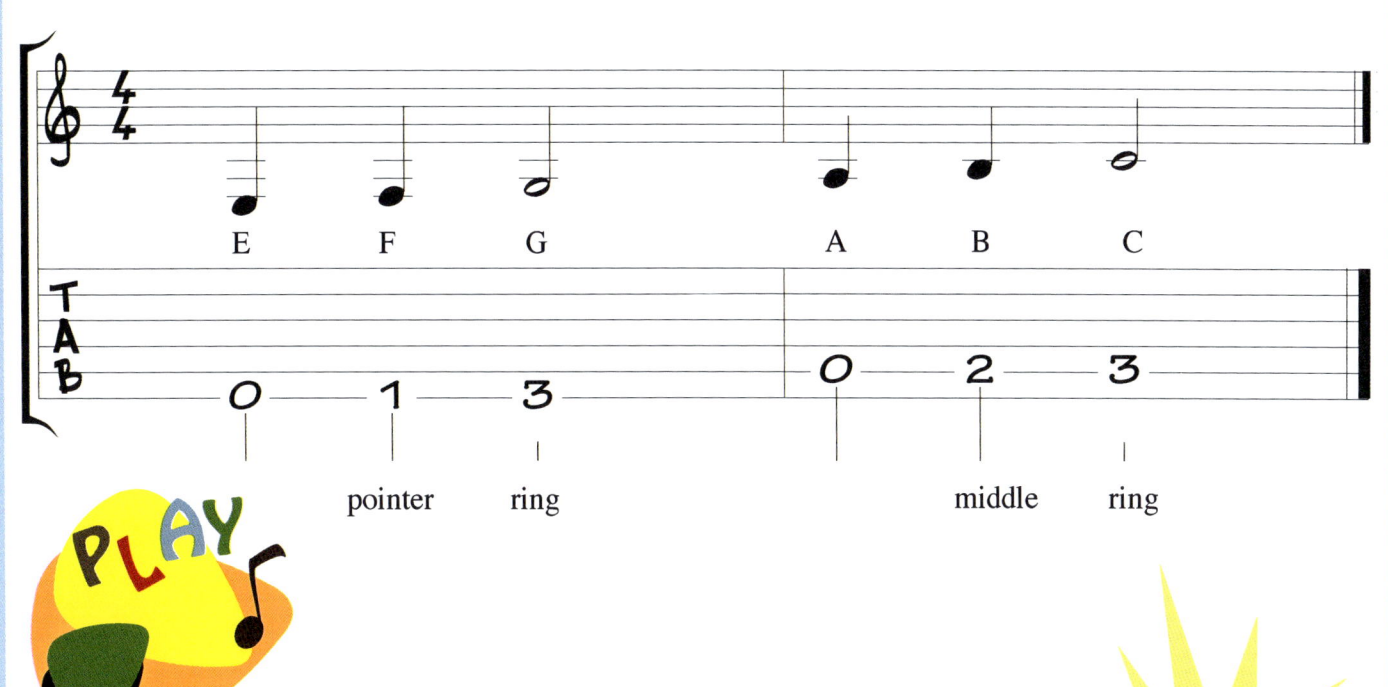

Super Duper Ball

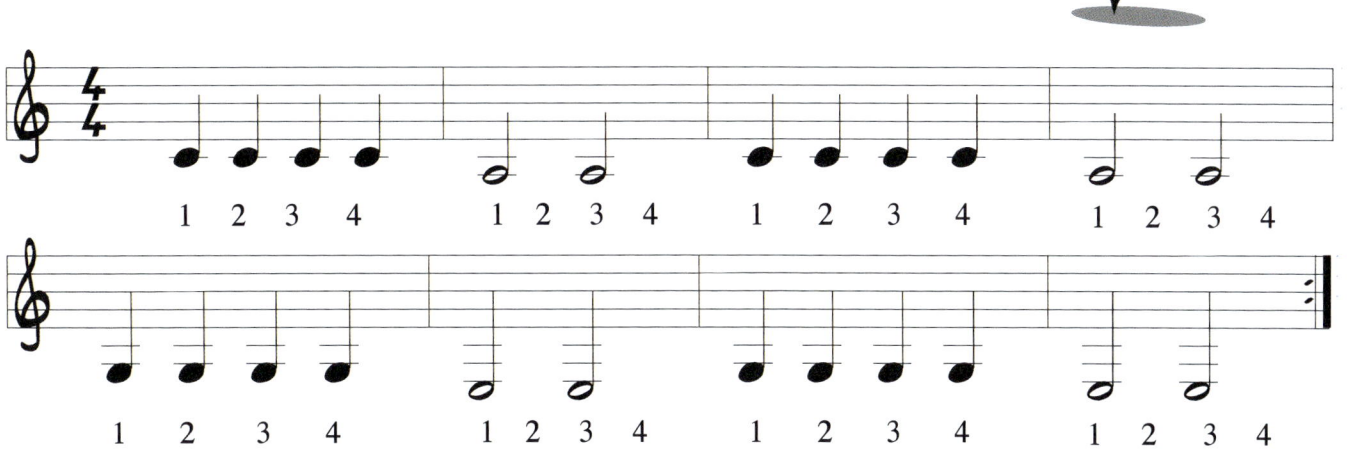

Test Your Knowledge

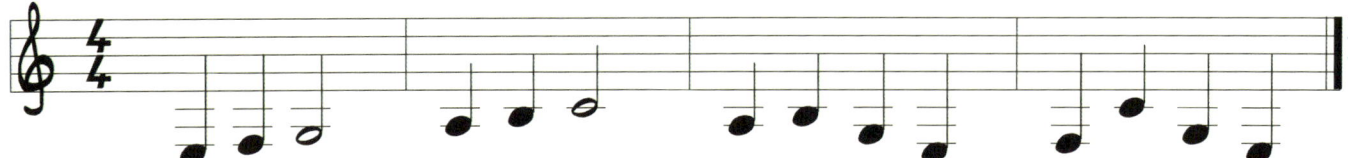

Write in the names of the notes in the spaces above.

Flamingo Finale

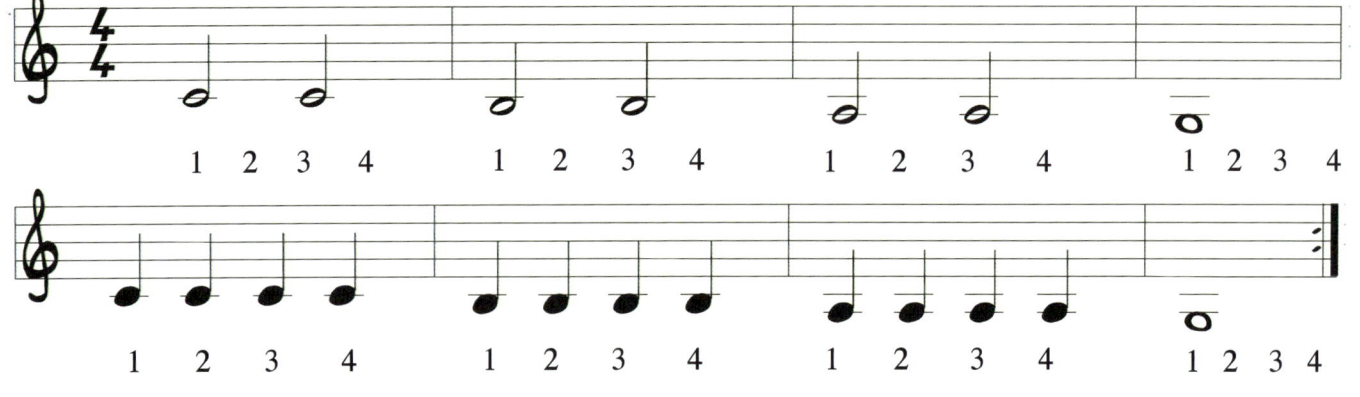

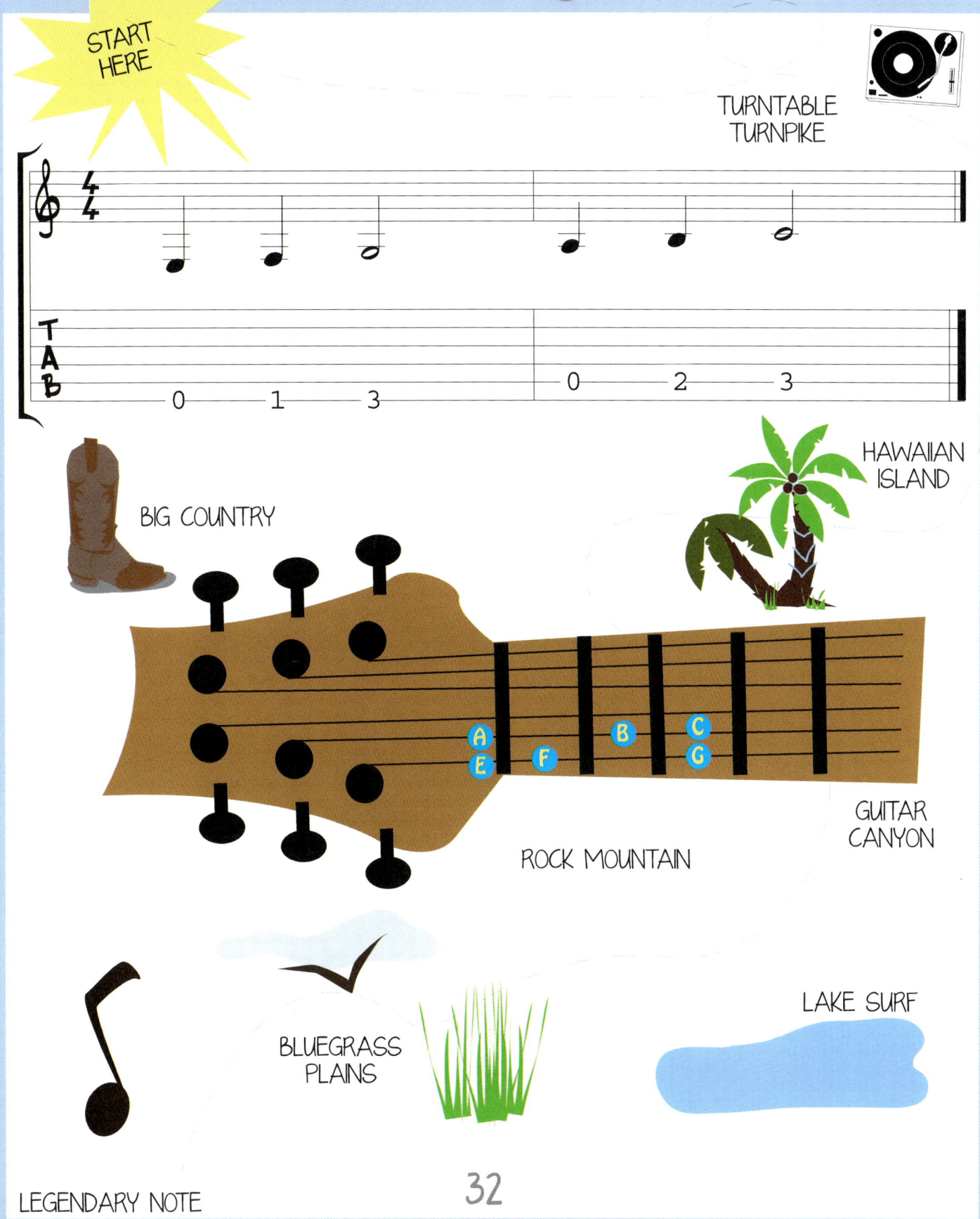

Congratulations!

Printed in Great Britain
by Amazon